BUTTERFLIES

NANCY J. SHAW

Creative Education

BUTTERFLY
TINIEST

The world's smallest butterfly is the western pygmy blue, with a wingspan of just half an inch. This North American butterfly is smaller than a dime.

4

Above, western pygmy blue; below, European skipper; right, malachite

Like the flowers of a garden, butterflies are many different shapes, sizes, and colors. They can be sunny yellow, shimmering blue, or bright orange, with the colors splashed in delicate patterns across their wings.

BUTTERFLIES AS INSECTS

Our world has nearly 20,000 different species, or kinds, of butterflies. These fascinating winged creatures have lived on earth for millions of years, and many people consider them to be among the most beautiful of all the world's **insects.**

Insects have six legs and three body parts: the head, the **thorax,** and the **abdomen.** Two pairs of large wings and the six legs are attached to the thorax, or middle body part.

Doris

BUTTERFLY
PREHISTORIC

Butterflies are very old insects. They have been flying on earth for at least 30 million years.

5

BUTTERFLY
S P E E D

A frightened butterfly can fly over 30 miles an hour and flap its wings 600 flaps a minute. Maybe that is why they are so hard to catch!

Above, small postman; right, great spangled fritillary

When butterflies land on flowers or leaves they often use only four legs and tuck their front two legs under their heads. Each slender leg is hinged in four sections, which allows the butterfly to bend and walk easily.

Butterflies have two large **compound eyes.** The butterfly can see in all directions at once because the compound eye is really thousands of tiny eyes formed together.

Two **antennae** are used to locate flowers and other butterflies. Their antennae, which act like noses, are sensitive to smells, are long and thin, and usually have a club at the end.

Butterflies also have a **proboscis,** a straw-like tongue that the butterfly keeps curled up under its head when not in use.

BUTTERFLY
N A M E

The name "butterfly" may have originated in England. Yellow butterflies, such as the English sulfur, probably reminded people of butter.

Below, common sulfur

BUTTERFLY
BITTER

Monarchs are very powerful fliers and taste bitter if eaten. Their bright orange color warns birds and other predators to stay away.

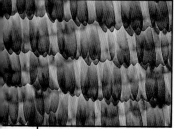

Above, butterfly wing scales; right, clipper

Butterflies resemble another insect, the moth, but there are several differences between the two. Butterflies fly during the day and are usually brightly colored, while most moths have dull-colored wings and are active during the night. The body of a butterfly is usually thin and hairless, while most moths have plump and furry bodies.

Butterflies belong to the insect group *Lepidoptera*, meaning scaly wings in Latin. No other insects except butterflies and moths have scales on their wings.

BUTTERFLY WINGS

Thousands of powder-like scales cover a butterfly's wings. These tiny scales overlap like rows of shingles on a roof and give the wings their color. Every time a butterfly flaps its wings, it loses some of its powdery scales. This is why older butterflies are often not as brightly colored as younger ones.

A butterfly's wings may look weak and fragile, but in fact they are very strong. The veins in their wings give them shape and support, just like the veins of a leaf.

M

The viceroy m *or copies, the pois* *nous monarch. Birds leave it alone because the viceroy looks just like its nasty-tasting cousin.*

Above, banded orange

of swall

BUTTERFLY

M I C

imics,

Every species of butterfly has a special wing shape that affects the way it flies. Some butterflies with large wings, such as swallowtails, flap and glide, while those with wide wings, such as the cabbage butterfly, flutter about in short bursts.

Butterflies with long, thin wings, such as the soaring birdwings, fly fast and straight. The short, triangular-shaped wings of the small skipper allow it to dart and "skip" about quickly.

BUTTERFLY HABITATS

Butterflies are found everywhere in the world except in Antarctica, where it is too cold for them to survive. Of the 20,000 species of butterflies in the world only about 700 species live in North America. Two of the largest and best known North American butterflies are the orange-and-black monarch and the yellow-and-black tiger swallowtail.

BUTTERF

BIGGEST

The Queen Alexandra's birdwing of the rain forests of Papua New Guinea is the largest known butterfly. Females have a wingspan of up to 11 inches (28 cm).

11

Left, tiger swallowtail

12

Above, camouflaged caterpillar resembling its food plant; top right, blue morpho; bottom right, gulf fritillary

The biggest and brightest butterflies in the world live in the warm tropical rain forests. In fact, more species of butterflies are found in the rain forests of Central and South America than anywhere else on earth. The brilliant blue morpho is one of the most spectacular rain forest butterflies. Its large wings reflect many different shades of blue in the tropical sunlight. Arctic butterflies, such as the clouded yellow butterfly and the fritillary, fly and feed only when the sun is shining.

Caterpillars of the giant birdwing butterflies are eaten as special treats by people in Papua New Guinea.

13

W hen it is cloudy, they seek shelter to stay warm. These butterflies have extra hairy bodies and "antifreeze" in their blood to keep from freezing to death in cooler weather.

Desert butterflies stay out of the sun and seek shelter in shady places. They fly in the early morning and in the cool evening. The little tiger blue and crimson tip butterflies of the Near East, and the African ringlet butterfly are desert survivors.

Left, mourning cloak; below, small tortoise-shell caterpillar

BUTTERFLY
HELPER

The painted lady lays her eggs on prickly thistle weeds. When the caterpillars hatch, they eat the thistles, which helps farmers control these pesky weeds.

Butterflies have learned to **adapt** to a variety of **habitats,** from the cold arctic to hot deserts. They can be found in high alpine meadows, in woodlands, grasslands, and wetlands.

Insects such as butterflies provide many animals, including birds, fish, frogs, and snakes, with an important food source.

Also, flowers and plants rely on butterflies for **pollination.** In their search for **nectar,** butterflies, like bees, carry pollen from flower to flower on their hairy bodies.

Wherever flowers are growing, these beautiful winged insects can be seen sipping nectar and fluttering about.

15

Far left, American painted lady; undersides of wings provide camouflage; left, American painted lady

BUTTERFLY

F A C T

Butterflies cannot fly when they are cold, so they open their wings to soak in the warmth of the sun before flying.

Right, red admiral; far right, zebra butterfly

WHAT BUTTERFLIES EAT

Most butterflies feed on a sweet liquid inside flower blossoms called nectar. As they fly from flower to flower, they use the taste pads on their feet to "taste" each blossom.

When they find an especially delicious flower, butterflies uncurl their proboscis into the blossom. They sip up the nectar just as you might drink milk through a straw. Flower nectar is the favorite food of butterflies, but some species also feed on tree sap and fruit.

BUTTERFLY
TRICKSTER

The mourning cloak pretends to be dead when approached by enemies. Then it makes a surprising "click" sound and flies away before it can be captured.

Above, mourning cloak drying wings after emerging from chrysalis; right, zebra butterflies roosting together

Butterflies often gather in groups on the sandy beach or by mud puddles as if they were sunbathing. Actually, they are drinking the water to gather the important salts and minerals that their bodies need.

HOW BUTTERFLIES REPRODUCE

All butterflies reproduce by laying eggs, but each species' egg is different in shape and markings from that of any other butterfly.

Butterflies attract their mates by color and wing patterns. They also release perfumed signals called **pheromones** when they are ready to mate. A pair of courting butterflies may flutter and dance around each other in the air for hours before mating.

BUTTERFLY
GARDEN

By planting nettles in your garden, you can attract peacock, comma, and red admiral butterflies, which lay their eggs on the nettle leaves.

Left, eggs of the zebra butterfly; above, peacock pansy

Butterflies cling to a plant and join abdomens to mate. They stay joined together for about an hour. After mating, the male flies off in search of another female, but the female of many species dies shortly after egg-laying.

Dozens or even hundreds of tiny eggs are laid on or near the "food plant" that the **larvae** will eat when they hatch. The female "glues" her eggs to the plant with a sticky substance from her abdomen.

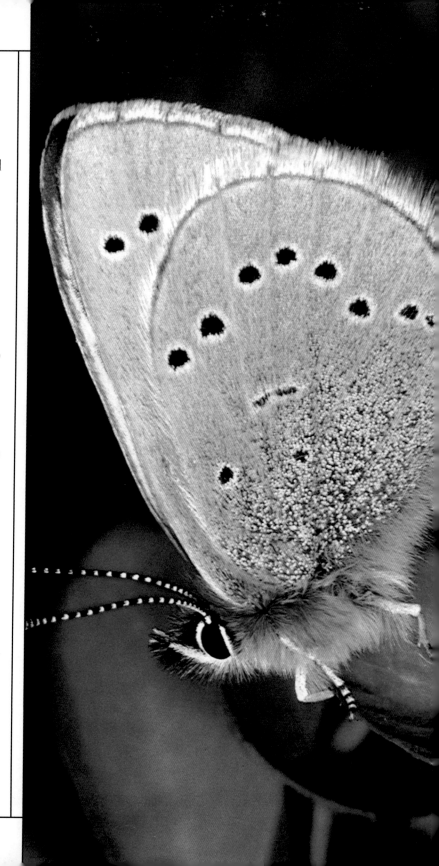

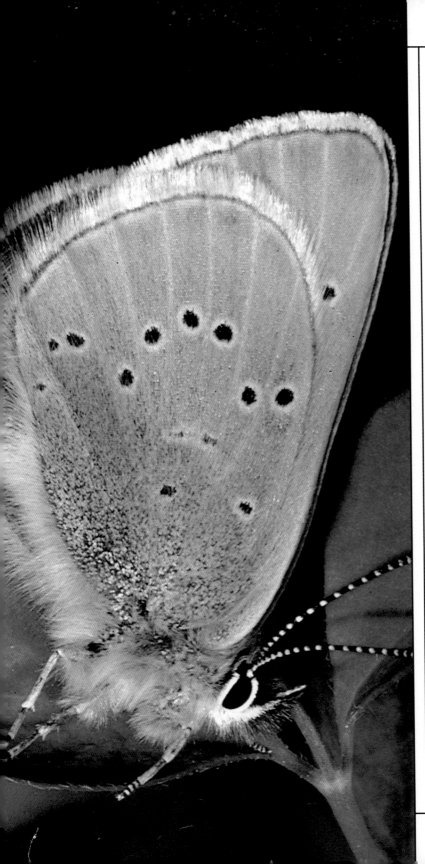

Some butterflies lay their eggs in clusters, while some species lay them one-by-one. Red admiral butterflies lay their eggs one-by-one on nettle leaves, and marbled white butterflies drop their eggs over the grass as they fly. Wherever the eggs fall, they stick.

How long it takes the eggs to hatch depends on the species of butterfly. Some eggs hatch within a few days. Others are laid in the fall but don't hatch until spring. All butterfly eggs are about the size of a pinhead.

BUTTERFLY
DISGUISE

The shape of the Indian leaf butterfly's brown wings protect it from predators; it looks just like an old torn leaf.

Left, silvery blues mating; above, Indian leaf

BUTTERFLY

FACT

The rice paper butterfly was named for its resemblance to the thin paper made of rice used in some Asian countries.

Above, rice paper; right, polydamas swallowtail caterpillar

BUTTERFLY LIFE CYCLE

When the egg hatches, the larva, called a **caterpillar,** crawls out and immediately begins eating the "food plant." The newly-hatched caterpillar, which has a tremendous appetite, grows fast.

Whenever the caterpillar's skin gets too tight, it splits open and the caterpillar crawls out of its old skin. Caterpillars may change their skin four or five times as they grow.

23

While the caterpillar is waiting for its new skin to harden, it stays very still to avoid being eaten by a hungry bird. To protect themselves, caterpillars use **camouflage** to blend in with their surroundings. Some caterpillars look like twigs or leaves; some even have sharp spines or prickly hairs. Many caterpillars, like the swallowtail, use bright colors to alert predators that they are poisonous. Others have large "fake eyes"—spots on their skin that fool an attacker into thinking the caterpillar is a large animal.

When the caterpillar is fully grown, it hangs upside down and attaches itself to a twig or leaf with a sticky liquid that comes from an opening near its mouth. Its body begins to change shape and the caterpillar sheds its skin for the last time.

Left, bright colors and spines mean poison! above, California dog-face butterfly

BUTTERFLY
TOWN

The city of Pacific Grove, California, known as "Butterfly Town U.S.A." is a popular resting place for migrating monarch butterflies.

Right, goliath birdwing emerging from chrysalis

Now the caterpillar has become a **pupa** resting inside a new tough shell called a **chrysalis.** During this stage in the life of the butterfly, the pupa changes into an adult. The length of the pupa stage and each stage in a butterfly's life cycle varies for each species.

The final stage of the butterfly's life cycle is the most incredible. When the adult insect pushes out of its chrysalis, an amazing change has occured. The adult looks nothing like a pupa or a caterpillar. It is a winged butterfly!

This amazing Transformation from egg, to caterpillar (larva), to pupa, to adult butterfly, is called **metamorphosis.** It is one of nature's greatest miracles.

After emerging from the chrysalis, the tired adult butterfly has wet and crumpled wings. It rests while its wings dry, flatten, and harden. After flapping and stretching its new wings to make them strong, the beautiful butterfly flutters off to begin the cycle of life again.

BUTTERFLY
LEGEND

The Ozark people of Arkansas once believed that whoever harmed the zebra swallowtail would have an accident causing blood to spill like the red "blood" spots on this butterfly's hind wings.

Above, zebra swallowtail

BUTTERFLY
MAGIC

Right, goliath birdwing; far right, postman

Tropical butterflies pass through all four stages of their life cycle more quickly than the butterflies of the temperate, or cooler climates. Adult tropical butterflies mate, lay eggs, and die, while the temperate butterflies may either **hibernate** or **migrate** to avoid freezing, living longer adult lives.

BUTTERFLY
V I S I O N

Butterflies can see all the colors of the rainbow and also ultraviolet light, which is a color that our human eyes cannot see.

28

Above, compound eye of the butterfly; top right, monarchs migrating; bottom right, American painted lady

MIGRATION

The migration patterns of butterflies have amazed and inspired people for hundreds of years. Century after century, certain species of butterflies, such as the monarch, have migrated south along the same routes, stopping in the same resting places along the way.

The painted lady travels up to 600 miles to spend the winter in warmer places, while some monarchs migrate up to 3,000 miles.

onarchs group together in swarms and can be seen by the thousands hanging on trees in the mountain forests of Mexico and in southern California. When spring brings warmer weather, the monarchs return north to mate and eventually die.

BUTTERFLY
F A C T

Crab spiders can change color to hide in flowers; when a butterfly comes to feed, it becomes the spider's meal!

Left, monarchs roosting; above, a crab spider approaching a zebulon skipper

BUTTERFLY SURVIVAL

Adult butterflies try to escape danger by quickly flying away from their enemies. But that doesn't always work, so they must rely on other methods of survival. Like caterpillars, they use many fascinating ways to warn their predators, such as hungry birds, frogs, spiders, and reptiles, to leave them alone. Some butterflies have false eyes that may startle a predator.

Camouflage also protects butterflies. When some butterfly species close their wings, they can easily blend in with their surroundings because the undersides of their wings are usually not brightly colored. Opening their wings with a sudden flash of bright color will often scare away a hungry attacker.

Right, trio of owl butterflies; far right, Malaysian lacewing

Butterflies are very sensitive to changes in their surroundings or environment. Scientists often discover new species of butterflies, but more often they discover that many species of butterflies are **endangered** or have become **extinct**.

Human destruction of butterfly habitats threatens the species living there. Pollution and pesticide use are also endangering many butterfly species worldwide. We need to be aware of the delicate balance of nature in which butterflies live and help protect their habitats.

Glossary

The **abdomen** is the last section of an insect body; it comes after the thorax.

When animals **adapt,** they change to become more suited to a changing environment.

The **antennae** are flexible, segmented sense organs on the head of an insect.

Camouflage is a way of hiding, by color or shape, and appearing to be part of the environment.

The wormlike, often brightly-colored, hairy or spiny larva of a butterfly is a **caterpillar.**

The **chrysalis** is the pupa of a butterfly or moth enclosed in a firm case or cocoon.

Compound eyes are made up of many light-sensitive parts that each form a portion of the image being viewed.

Endangered animals are threatened with becoming so few in number that their kind will become **extinct,** dying out completely and disappearing from the earth.

Habitats are the places where animals or plants naturally live and grow.

Animals that **hibernate** pass the cold winter in a state of inactivity, often sleeping and not eating.

Insects are small animals of the class *Insecta*; in their adult stage they have three pairs of legs and a body segmented into head, thorax, and abdomen, and usually two pairs of wings.

Before their adult stage, insects such as butterflies are wingless, wormlike **larvae.**

When animals change, as butterflies change from larvae to adult, they go through a **metamorphosis.**

Animals that **migrate** travel from one location to another, usually because of changes in the seasons.

The sweet liquid secreted by flowers is called **nectar;** it makes good food for many insects.

Pheromones are chemicals secreted by animals to affect the behavior of other animals of its own kind.

Pollination is the transfer of pollen from one plant to another; pollination is needed for plants to reproduce.

The slender, tube-shaped feeding organ of butterflies is called the **proboscis.**

A butterfly or moth larva undergoes a complete transformation within a chrysalis, becoming a **pupa;** this is the stage before adulthood.

The **thorax** is the second, or middle part of the body of an insect; it comes after the head.